CALLIDORA

GLOBAL MEDIA

Published in the United States of America
By Callidora Global Media, LLC

ISBN: 979-8-218-72397-2

Printed and bound in the United States of America and other countries
by IngramSpark and its partners.

HOW TO ENJOY WORK WHEN YOU HATE YOUR JOB

TJ MINSON, M.A.

DEDICATION

For the unyielding spirit within you: for every person who refuses to let circumstances define their worth.

May you come to see that the right mindset, steady belief, and bold action are the keys to overcoming anything. This job is not your destiny; it is a chapter, a challenge, and a chance to become a stronger, truer version of yourself.

When you embrace that truth, you rise, and in doing so, help others rise with you.

CONTENTS

PREFACE

I've always been curious about what drives people to care, perform, and stay committed at work, and what happens when that energy starts to fade. I've seen smart, capable professionals disengage quietly, not because they lacked ability, but because no one took the time to ask what mattered to them. I've seen high performers rewarded with more work while others coasted by because of who they knew or mastered the shell game of looking busy. I've seen priorities shift without explanation and accountability applied unevenly. These patterns wear people down. Over time, they stop aiming to be great and start trying to survive.

That frustration became fuel. I earned a Master's in Organizational Leadership with a focus on Training and Development because I wanted to understand people more deeply. Not just what they do, but why. I've always been fascinated by psychology, but I knew I wanted to stay rooted in the business world. Organizational Leadership felt like the right bridge. It was more human than an MBA, more focused on real dynamics inside organizations, and more aligned with how I wanted to lead. It wasn't about titles. It was about learning how to actually make work better.

I've always believed that leadership means learning what motivates your team, what their goals are, and what they're carrying behind the scenes. It means understanding that work affects identity, family, health, and self-worth. It means knowing that the people are the company. Without them, nothing exists.

For me, motivation was never just about money, though financial pressure played a role. It was about leveling up and changing the story for my family. I was the first in my family to graduate from college, then to earn a master's degree. That decision shifted everything, not just for me, but for the people watching. It inspired my sister to pursue her own path. She went on to earn not one but two degrees. That legacy matters to me. So does the responsibility that comes with it.

This book began as a capstone project in 2011. It looked at the roots of disengagement, identity loss at work, and the invisible weight that builds when people feel unseen. At the time, I didn't know it would grow into something more. But I kept learning. I watched what happened when leadership showed up, and when it didn't. I saw how poor management decisions could hollow out an entire team, and how thoughtful, grounded leadership could bring people back to life.

Over the years, I saw more and more people quietly check out of their jobs. It wasn't laziness. It wasn't entitlement. It was frustration with systems that rarely listen, rarely change, and rarely value people beyond what they produce. The rise of quiet quitting wasn't surprising. It was overdue. That shift in the workplace is what finally pushed me to finish this book. I knew the timing mattered. I knew people needed words for what they were experiencing and a way to move forward without burning out or giving in.

What you'll find in these pages isn't motivational fluff or performative advice. It's honest reflection shaped by real work, lived observation, and a deep respect for the people trying to hold it together in environments that rarely return the favor.

If you've ever felt disconnected from the work you do or the culture around you, this book will feel familiar. If you've been asking yourself whether it's you or the system, this book will help you answer that without shame. And if you've ever stayed longer than you should have, not out of weakness but because the bills were real and the options were few, this book will not judge you for it.

This isn't about blame. It's about clarity. You deserve to understand what's really happening so you can protect your energy and move forward without apology.

Let's start there. ◆

INTRODUCTION

You've just heard a bit of my story. Now let's talk about why so many people are reaching their breaking point, and why this book meets them at that moment.

This book is for the professionals who work hard, care deeply, and still lie awake at night wondering if any of it is worth it. It's for the ones who keep showing up even when the job no longer feels like a fit and the culture asks for more than it gives back. What you'll find in these pages isn't speculation. It's informed by lived experience, extensive research, and deep engagement with the psychological and cultural shifts shaping the workplace today.

I've had a front-row seat to what happens when leadership goes right and when it doesn't. I've watched people rise not because they led well, but because they performed for power, focused solely on kissing ass or hiring only friends, even if they weren't qualified. I've seen entire teams unravel under the weight of ego-driven decision-making, making false promises and then covering their tracks, while others quietly thrived under leaders who understood how to build trust, not just manage perception, who didn't take shortcuts and led with integrity. Maybe you're thinking of a few names right now. It shows it's an epidemic.

These contrasts shaped how I think about integrity, accountability, and power at work. Real leadership, I've come to believe, isn't solely about authority. It's about telling the truth, even when it's uncomfortable. It's about adapting to the situation, the person, and the team without ego. It's about honoring the people who show up every day not for applause, but because they believe in something bigger than a job title. Sure, they do it for the money, we all do, but I'm talking about fulfillment.

The best leaders aren't intimidated by talent or visibility. They don't suppress the talent for fear of losing their own jobs. They create space for people to thrive. They know that a company's true value isn't found in politics, optics, or the same cliques rotating under different logos. It's in the people who contribute with purpose and consistency, whether or not they get credit.

One of the most revealing aspects of writing this book has been realizing that the people I've worked with across industries and levels will likely see themselves.

The ones who led with purpose will feel it. The ones who clung to self-preservation, ego, or control will feel that too.

This isn't a guide to burning it all down. But it is a call to get honest about what's working, what's not, and what needs to shift before you lose more of yourself trying to hold it all together.

Whether you're burned out, quietly questioning your next move, or just ready to think more critically about how work fits into your life, this book meets you exactly where you are.

We're living in a time when burnout, quiet quitting, and mental health challenges are no longer rare. They're everywhere. People want more than just a paycheck. They want purpose, psychological safety, and work that doesn't erode their sense of self. The desire for meaningful, honest work isn't a trend. It's a reckoning.

Inside, you'll find practical insights grounded in academic research, real stories, and the voices of thinkers like Maslow, Frankl, Bandura, and Brené Brown. You'll also see data from Gallup, WHO, and McKinsey. But more than that, you'll find lived truth, the kind you only get by walking through it.

We'll talk about how overpromising from leadership, even when well-intentioned, chips away at culture. Unmet expectations don't just bruise morale. They plant quiet disillusionment that spreads fast. Once that sets in, even the best people start to disengage.

The tone here is direct, but not cynical. It's sharp, but never bitter. This isn't about blame. It's about understanding the landscape so you can move forward with more clarity, more self-trust, and a lot less noise.

What This Book Is About

This book explores what happens when work begins to wear down your energy, confidence, or sense of direction and how to restore your power without having to start from scratch.

You'll learn:

- Why we stay in roles that don't work anymore
- What fear, stress, and burnout do to your decision-making
- How loyalty and performance culture shape self-worth
- What it takes to hold boundaries and still stay employed
- How to find meaning in imperfect roles

You'll find a blend of research, reflection, and personal narrative, all intended to help you make sense of your own experience and feel grounded in what comes next. The tone is honest but not hopeless, practical but not detached. It's written with a clear understanding of how complex work can be and how powerful people can become when they understand their own patterns and values more clearly.

Why Emotional Truth Still Matters

You don't need platitudes. You need thoughtful insight from someone who understands the realities of modern work and has done the research to back it up. This book won't deny how complicated work can be, especially for people who care deeply, perform consistently, and still feel the cost of constant adaptation.

But it also won't leave you there. The goal isn't to dwell. The goal is to equip, to give you tools, language, and perspective that help you take back control. Not overnight, but steadily. Intentionally. With less fear and more self-trust.

Let's begin there. Not with perfection. Not with certainty. But with something far better: clarity, and the capacity to choose how you want to lead your own work life, from the inside out. ◆

CHAPTER 1

Why We Stay,
Even When We're Miserable

"The idea of enjoying work may sound like a luxury. However, for many, it has become a psychological necessity."

If you have ever looked around at your coworkers and silently wondered, "Are we all just pretending to be okay?" you are not imagining things.

For many people, work has become less about purpose and more about emotional survival. We show up tired. We log in exhausted. We navigate stress, uncertainty, and disengagement while pretending everything is fine. Beneath the surface, something deeper is happening. People are pushing themselves to keep functioning in environments that are no longer functional, often without a clear strategy for how to regain their footing.

The idea of enjoying work may sound like a luxury. However, for many, it has become a psychological necessity.

In 1943, psychologist Abraham Maslow introduced the Hierarchy of Needs, a framework that positioned human motivation as a progressive set of requirements. According to Maslow, individuals must first satisfy foundational needs such as physical safety and emotional belonging before they can pursue higher aspirations like meaning, growth, or creativity (Maslow, 1943). This concept remains relevant in modern work culture. If someone feels emotionally unsafe at work, the problem is not attitude. It is a disruption of psychological safety at a foundational level.

Over the past fifteen years, the conditions of modern work have shifted dramatically. The 2008 global financial crisis destabilized job markets across sectors and caused widespread layoffs and economic contraction. Twelve years later, the COVID-19 pandemic accelerated workplace transformation on a global scale. Millions of workers lost jobs. Entire industries paused or disappeared. Remote work became the norm almost overnight. These events were not isolated. Together, they reshaped expectations, disrupted any illusion of long-term job security, and exposed the fragility of systems that once felt permanent.

The promises once tied to employment such as security, advancement, and reward have often proven unpredictable or inaccessible. The equation we were taught was simple. Work hard, deliver results, and success would follow. For many, that has not held true, prompting a need for a new approach to professional fulfillment.

According to Gallup's 2023 *Global Workplace Report*, only 23 percent of employees worldwide report being engaged in their work (Gallup, 2023).

Gallup defines engagement as the involvement and enthusiasm of employees in their work and workplace. That means more than three out of four workers are emotionally disconnected or actively disengaged. When engagement disappears, so does motivation, satisfaction, and a sense of value.

People stay in jobs that drain them for many reasons.

Some are practical, like income, health insurance, visa sponsorship, childcare, or the need to keep food on the table. Others are emotional, such as fear of change, loyalty to colleagues, a sense of obligation, or the belief that things might improve. Some workers feel pressure to appear committed, strong, or grateful. Others cannot imagine starting over.

It is common to tell ourselves, "This is just what adult life feels like." That belief is understandable, but resignation is not the same as resilience.

You are not weak for feeling worn down. You are not broken for needing more than a paycheck. When someone spends enough time in an unhealthy system, the body often recognizes the damage before the mind is ready to accept it.

This book is not about encouraging people to walk out dramatically or start over without a plan. It is about reclaiming agency. That begins with understanding what is happening both around you and within you.

People deserve work that does not leave them feeling hollow. They deserve leadership that fosters trust instead of fear. They deserve a culture that honors their humanity, not just their productivity.

Not everyone can leave a difficult job immediately. Some cannot leave at all. Every person still deserves tools that help them stay without losing themselves.

In his 1841 essay *Self-Reliance*, Ralph Waldo Emerson wrote, "To be yourself in a world that is constantly trying to make you something else is the greatest accomplishment"(Emerson, 1841).

This idea still resonates. It matters especially in professional spaces where performance is prioritized over people.

There is a path to dignity, even when the work itself feels depleting. There is a way to reconnect with value, even in environments that feel transactional. The goal is not to tolerate dysfunction. It is to recognize it, name it, and decide how to move forward with clarity. Let us begin there. ◆

CHAPTER 2

When Quitting Isn't an Option

"If your body feels tired all the time, there is a reason. If your motivation has disappeared, that is data. If your anxiety spikes the moment your boss's name appears in your inbox, that is not just stress. That is a warning."

Quitting is often romanticized as the ultimate act of self-respect. Walk away. Reclaim your peace. Choose yourself. In theory, it sounds simple.

In reality, most people cannot just leave a job the moment it becomes emotionally or mentally damaging. Financial responsibilities remain. Health insurance does not wait. Children still need care. Mortgage and rent still come due. For millions of workers, the option to walk away is not a choice. It is a privilege they do not currently have.

That does not mean they are stuck forever. It means that advice like "just quit" ignores the complexity of real life. It dismisses practical and psychological realities. It fails to account for what it takes to survive inside a system that is no longer working.

You might not be there because you want to be. You're there because, for now, you have to be.

When you cannot change your external situation, the only power you have is how you respond internally. That does not mean pretending things are fine. It means learning how to protect your energy while quietly preparing for change.

The American Psychological Association defines chronic workplace stress as a condition in which the demands of a job exceed a person's ability to cope. Left unmanaged, it can lead to physical symptoms, emotional exhaustion, sleep problems, and long-term health issues. These are not overreactions. They are physiological red flags.

If your body feels tired all the time, there is a reason. If your motivation has disappeared, that is data. If your anxiety spikes the moment your boss's name appears in your inbox, that is not just stress. That is a warning.

While you are still in the job, there are ways to reduce further emotional damage. These steps will not fix a toxic system, but they can help you stay grounded until you are ready to leave.

1. Create Micro-Boundaries
You may not be able to overhaul your schedule, but you can protect small moments. Silence notifications after hours. Take your lunch without apology. Stop over-explaining yourself. These actions reclaim just enough space to remind you that your time is still yours.

2. Track the Truth
Gaslighting thrives in confusion. Keep a private log of emails, events,

and conversations that feel off. Not for HR. For your own clarity. It affirms that your memory is trustworthy, even if your environment tries to distort it.

3. Preserve Your Identity Outside of Work
When your job becomes your only source of value, it can distort your entire sense of self. Reconnect with who you are outside of your role. Invest in routines, people, or hobbies that remind you that your worth is not tied to your badge, title or inbox.

4. Reconnect with Purpose
Even in difficult roles, your values still matter. Maybe you care about doing quality work. Maybe you show up because your team relies on you. Locate that thread of integrity and hold it without letting the system define it for you.

5. Build Your Exit Strategy
This may not be fast. It might not even be linear. Begin anyway. Update your resume. Research roles. Learn what is possible. Give yourself something to move toward instead of simply running from what hurts.

Staying in a harmful environment does not mean you have failed. It means you are managing a complex reality with the tools and responsibilities you have. That takes resilience. It also takes emotional discipline.

In *Man's Search for Meaning*, psychiatrist Viktor Frankl wrote, "When we are no longer able to change a situation, we are challenged to change ourselves" (Frankl, 1959).

This is not about passive acceptance. It is about reclaiming control where it still exists, even if the situation remains difficult.

You are allowed to feel tired. You are allowed to hate your job and still do it well. You are allowed to preserve your energy without guilt. These truths can coexist.

Leaving is not the only way to demonstrate strength. Sometimes, continuing without breaking is its own form of power. ◆

CHAPTER 3

When Work Steals Your Confidence

"Some jobs develop your skills. Others dismantle your confidence. The problem is that by the time you notice the damage, it has already taken root."

Some jobs develop your skills. Others dismantle your confidence. The problem is that by the time you notice the damage, it has already taken root.

Confidence erosion at work is not always obvious. It often begins subtly. You hesitate before speaking. You second-guess decisions you used to make without hesitation. You apologize more than necessary. Eventually, you begin to shrink yourself to fit the dysfunction.

Toxic workplaces do not just harm morale. They reshape identity.

Psychologist Albert Bandura, in his foundational research on self-efficacy, described how a person's belief in their ability to succeed shapes how they think, behave, and feel. When that belief is consistently undermined, both performance and emotional resilience decline (Bandura, 1977). This erosion can be slow and insidious. It is particularly destructive in environments where people receive conflicting signals such as encouragement followed by criticism or inclusion followed by exclusion.

The damage compounds in cultures that reward silence over contribution, compliance over creativity, or emotional suppression over honest communication.

If you have ever left a meeting feeling invisible despite your preparation, or watched less qualified peers move ahead because they are louder or more agreeable, the issue is not your value. It is the system's failure to recognize it.

Confidence theft often looks like:

- Being excluded from key conversations while still being expected to execute
- Receiving vague or contradictory feedback without clear direction
- Being consistently talked over, corrected, or minimized
- Watching your work credited to someone else
- Being told you are "too sensitive" or "not a team player" for raising valid concerns

These experiences do more than affect productivity. They distort self perception.

Over time, people internalize the dysfunction. They begin to believe they are the problem. They question their worth. They stop speaking up or advocating for themselves. Eventually, they stop trying altogether. This often happens not from apathy, but from exhaustion. Proving your value to a system that refuses to acknowledge it becomes emotionally unsustainable.

This is the point where the rebuilding begins.

Confidence is not arrogance. It is not performance. It is a quiet knowing that you are capable, even when external affirmation is lacking.

If your job has led you to doubt this, here are truths worth remembering:

1. Your Skills Still Matter
The dysfunction around you does not erase your competence. It only clouds your ability to see it clearly.

2. You Are Not Too Much
Feedback that is delivered with judgment or wrapped in bias is not mentorship. You do not need to dilute your personality to earn inclusion.

3. You Are Allowed to Advocate for Yourself
Even if the workplace discourages it. Even if it makes people uncomfortable. Your voice matters.

4. Your Self-Worth Is Not Defined by a Manager's Opinion
Authority is not the same as insight. Power does not equal truth.

In *The Gifts of Imperfection*, researcher Brené Brown wrote, "Let go of who you think you're supposed to be. Embrace who you are" (Brown, 2010).

That advice may feel radical in a workplace that punishes authenticity. But it is essential. You cannot heal while pretending that nothing is wrong.

You may have learned to survive in a dysfunctional culture. You may have learned to stay quiet, keep your head down, and avoid drawing attention. Those habits were protective. They helped you endure.

However, survival mode is not meant to be permanent.

Confidence can be rebuilt. Even after long periods of erosion. It begins by separating your value from the behavior of the people around you. It grows when you choose to surround yourself with people who see you accurately, not through the lens of workplace dysfunction.

What you're capable of isn't limited to what this job ever allowed you to show. You're allowed to remember who you were before you began questioning your worth. ◆

CHAPTER 4

The Emotional Cost of
Pretending You're Fine

"Pretending to be fine at work is one of the most exhausting performances a person can maintain. It is the silent agreement many professionals make with themselves to keep the peace, avoid scrutiny, or simply get through the day."

Pretending to be fine at work is one of the most exhausting performances a person can maintain. It is the silent agreement many professionals make with themselves to keep the peace, avoid scrutiny, or simply get through the day.

You show up, smile politely, nod in meetings, and tell your manager everything is going well. Inside, you feel depleted. This disconnect between outer behavior and inner truth creates a quiet form of psychological fatigue.

The longer you pretend, the more distant you become from yourself.

This experience is not just emotional. It is physiological. According to the American Institute of Stress, chronic emotional suppression can lead to elevated cortisol, disrupted sleep cycles, impaired immune function, and even cardiovascular complications (American Institute of Stress, n.d.). Your body records the stress even when your words deny it.

There are times when the mask serves a purpose. You do not owe your vulnerability to your employer. Boundaries are valid. However, when pretending becomes habitual, it exacts a cost.

Emotional disconnection often manifests in subtle but powerful ways:

- Irritability over minor inconveniences
- Apathy toward tasks that once felt purposeful
- Exhaustion after routine interactions
- Emotional numbness where pride or ambition used to live

You begin to forget what genuine engagement feels like. You drift into a kind of emotional autopilot, completing tasks but rarely connecting to them.

Organizational psychologists refer to this as surface acting, which means expressing emotions you do not genuinely feel in order to meet professional expectations. Research published in the *Journal of Applied Psychology* shows that prolonged surface acting correlates with higher levels of burnout, lower job satisfaction, and greater turnover (Hülsheger & Schewe, 2011).

You are not just tired. You are exhausted from operating without authenticity.

It is easy to dismiss this experience. You may find yourself saying things like, "I should be grateful," or "Others have it worse," or "This is just how it is." These thoughts are common. They are also frequently inaccurate.

You do not need a dramatic event to justify your fatigue. Persistent emotional misalignment is reason enough.

In her book *Radical Acceptance*, psychologist Tara Brach writes, "The boundary to what we can accept is the boundary to our freedom" (Brach, 2003).

The moment you stop denying how drained you feel is the moment you begin to restore your emotional energy.

This does not mean disclosing your private struggles to everyone at work. It means no longer gaslighting yourself into silence.

Here are a few ways to reconnect with your emotional truth:

1. Tell Yourself the Truth in Private
No filters. No spin. Write down what you feel. Say it aloud. Let it be real.

2. Notice Your Energy Leaks
Pay attention to when you start performing. Ask yourself who you are protecting and what you fear would happen if you stopped.

3. Create Space for Authentic Connection
Find someone you trust. You do not need advice. You need reflection. A single honest conversation can interrupt isolation.

4. Let Small Honesty Return
You do not have to announce burnout in a staff meeting. You can respond to, "How are you?" with, "Honestly, this week has been tough." Truth builds trust, even in small amounts.

The long-term goal is not just to pretend less. It is to live in a way where pretending becomes less necessary.

That starts with internal honesty, even if external conditions remain rigid. You are not fragile for feeling fatigued by performance. You are perceptive for noticing the emotional cost.

People were not built to wear masks indefinitely. Over time, the mask cracks or the person beneath it begins to fade.

Pretending drains more than it protects. Telling the truth, even gently, begins the return to wholeness. ◆

CHAPTER 5

When Coworkers Become the Problem

"Workplace betrayal rarely arrives with a warning. It often hides behind a smile, a Slack emoji, or a "Just following up" email."

Some of the deepest workplace wounds do not come from supervisors. They come from peers.

Coworkers are supposed to be allies, collaborators, and occasional sources of camaraderie. In many cases, they are. But in toxic environments, even peer relationships can turn into strategic battlegrounds.

It starts subtly. Someone interrupts you in a meeting. A colleague fails to credit your input. A teammate suddenly withholds information, creating confusion you are expected to fix. You begin to wonder if you are imagining things.

Over time, the subtle shifts become patterns.

Workplace betrayal rarely arrives with a warning. It often hides behind a smile, a Slack emoji, or a "Just following up" email. The damage is not only in the act itself but in the disorientation that follows. You thought someone was a teammate. Then you discover they were positioning themselves to move ahead at your expense.

This is not about office drama. It is about survival instincts in environments where collaboration is preached but competition is rewarded.

According to research from the *Academy of Management Journal*, employees in competitive environments are more likely to withhold information, sabotage colleagues, and engage in "social undermining" when resources like promotions, praise, or visibility are scarce (Duffy et al., 2002). In these workplaces, trust erodes and self-protection replaces teamwork.

If any of this feels familiar, you are not paranoid. You are picking up on real dynamics.

Coworker betrayal can look like:

- Taking credit for your work or ideas
- Withholding information that affects your performance
- Shifting blame for mistakes
- Performing empathy in public while undermining you in private
- Forming exclusionary cliques or gossip cycles

These experiences are not just frustrating. They are emotionally disorienting. You may find yourself replaying interactions, second-guessing your instincts, or minimizing what happened to avoid the discomfort of naming it.

If your workplace also discourages conflict or favors "positivity" over accountability, speaking up becomes even harder. You begin to feel like the problem simply for noticing one exists.

Here is the truth. You are not overreacting when you feel hurt by peer dynamics. Psychological safety is not only about how managers treat you. It also includes how you are treated by the people you work alongside every day.

So what can you do?

1. Name It Privately
You do not need to confront someone right away. Start by writing out the situation with specifics. This helps you see the pattern more clearly and reduces self-gaslighting.

2. Document Objectively
Keep a record of key incidents. Use neutral language. Focus on facts. If a pattern emerges, you will have data, not just emotion.

3. Set Boundaries Where You Can
You may not control someone else's behavior, but you can reduce your exposure. Decline nonessential meetings. Limit casual collaboration. Protect your energy.

4. Focus on Work Visibility
Make your contributions traceable. Summarize conversations over email. Recap your ideas in writing. Create a paper trail that affirms your role without sounding defensive.

5. Choose Allies Intentionally
Find one or two trusted colleagues who value integrity. You do not need a group. You need consistency. A single trusted voice can restore perspective.

Betrayal hurts more when it comes from people you once trusted. That does not make you weak. It makes you human. The goal is not to become cynical. The goal is to stay steady.

In environments where image often overshadows impact, protecting your professionalism does not mean suppressing the truth. It means using discernment.

As Maya Angelou once said, "When someone shows you who they are, believe them the first time" (Angelou, 1986).

You do not need to respond to every slight. You do need to protect your peace.

When coworkers become part of the problem, emotional clarity becomes part of your strategy. ◆

CHAPTER 6

When the Culture Is a Lie

"The most dangerous workplace cultures are not always overtly hostile. They are often performative. They present as friendly while masking fear, dysfunction, or power imbalances underneath. They praise transparency while punishing dissent. They celebrate resilience while ignoring chronic burnout."

Company culture is supposed to be the invisible glue that holds an organization together. It shapes behavior, drives priorities, and defines what people believe they are part of. In theory, it is the foundation of trust, collaboration, and pride.

In practice, it is often just branding.

You have seen the signs. "We're like a family here." "We care about people, not just profits." "We lead with empathy." These phrases appear in onboarding packets, team meetings, and recruitment posts. But when you compare the words to the daily experience, something does not add up.

A positive culture should show up in how people treat one another. It should be felt in how feedback is given, how boundaries are honored, and how problems are handled. It should not require a hashtag.

The most dangerous workplace cultures are not always overtly hostile. They are often performative. They present as friendly while masking fear, dysfunction, or power imbalances underneath. They praise transparency while punishing dissent. They celebrate resilience while ignoring chronic burnout.

You are not imagining it if you feel out of place in a culture that looks good on paper but feels hollow in reality.

According to the *Harvard Business Review*, organizational culture becomes toxic when values are inconsistent, behaviors are misaligned, and leadership tolerates dysfunction (Gorbatov & Lane, 2020). Culture is not defined by mission statements. It is defined by what gets rewarded and what gets ignored.

If gossip is tolerated, that is the culture.

If favoritism drives advancement, that is the culture.

If burnout is ignored and silence is praised, that is the culture.

You may find yourself second-guessing your instincts. You wonder if you are being negative or if you just do not fit. This is not about fit. It is about truth.

You are not difficult for noticing what others have normalized. You are observant.

When culture and reality do not match, trust erodes. Engagement drops. People stop offering ideas, not because they have none, but because they have learned it is safer to stay quiet.

Here are signs that your company culture may be more illusion than substance:

- Leaders only engage during crises or reviews
- Feedback is one-directional, rarely invited from below
- Recognition is selective and political
- Diversity is used as a photo, not a priority
- Conflict is avoided in favor of "keeping the peace"

When you cannot trust the culture, you begin managing risk instead of doing your best work.

So what can you do when the stated culture is disconnected from the lived experience?

1. Stop Internalizing the Gap
The culture's failure to reflect its stated values is not your personal failure. You do not need to work harder to force a sense of belonging.

2. Observe Without Excusing
Notice what gets rewarded. Notice what gets overlooked. Let that guide how you show up. Not everything needs your full emotional investment.

3. Protect Your Values
You cannot control the culture, but you can choose what you embody. Operate with clarity and professionalism, even when others do not.

4. Reassess Your Fit
This is not about blame. It is about alignment. If the values you care about most are missing or misused, it is okay to start exploring what comes next.

The truth is, many organizations rely on aspirational language while avoiding the hard work of cultural accountability. That does not mean all cultures are lies. It means some have become theater.

You are not asking for too much when you want consistency between what is said and what is practiced. You are asking for honesty.

In *The Culture Code*, Daniel Coyle writes, "Real culture is not something you declare. It is something you build, together, every day" (Coyle, 2018).

Culture is not a slogan. It is a lived experience. If the experience is causing harm, the language does not redeem it.

You do not have to stay in places that contradict your values. You also do not have to make a dramatic exit. Clarity is power. The sooner you stop pretending the culture matches the branding, the sooner you can make decisions rooted in truth. ◆

CHAPTER 7

The Loyalty Illusion

"Loyalty is often praised as a virtue in the workplace. It sounds noble. Commitment. Dedication. Being a team player. But in many organizations, loyalty is quietly repurposed as a tool for control."

Loyalty is often praised as a virtue in the workplace. It sounds noble. Commitment. Dedication. Being a team player. But in many organizations, loyalty is quietly repurposed as a tool for control.

The message is rarely stated directly. Instead, it is implied through norms and reinforced through repetition. Do not rock the boat. Do not question authority. Do not talk about what is not working. Just be grateful to have a job and keep your head down.

This is not loyalty. It is silent compliance.

A healthy workplace earns loyalty through integrity, fairness, and consistency. A toxic workplace demands loyalty through fear, guilt, or manipulation. You are expected to go above and beyond, often without acknowledgment, while being told that raising concerns reflects poorly on your character.

If you have ever hesitated to speak up because you worried it would make you seem ungrateful, disloyal, or "not a team player," you are not alone. That hesitation is a learned response to a culture that prioritizes comfort over accountability.

Loyalty becomes dangerous when it is only expected in one direction.

Research published in the *Journal of Organizational Behavior* highlights that "perceived organizational support" is essential to employee well-being and retention. When employees feel their contributions are valued and their needs matter, they are more likely to remain engaged and committed (Eisenberger et al., 2002). Loyalty without reciprocity creates resentment.

Some of the most toxic workplaces are held together by the emotional weight of loyalty. People stay because they care about their team, feel connected to their clients, or have invested years into building something they hoped would grow. These attachments are real. So is the damage when they are exploited.

You may begin to tell yourself, "It would be worse somewhere else," or "I owe it to the people here," or "This is just how leadership works." These rationalizations may help you cope temporarily. Eventually, they become a trap.

You are not disloyal for questioning dysfunction. You are discerning.

You can care about your work and still recognize when it is hurting you. You can value your colleagues and still choose to set boundaries. You can love parts of your role and still outgrow the environment.

Here are signs that your workplace may be using loyalty as leverage:

- Loyalty is praised only when it results in silence or overwork
- Speaking up is met with defensiveness or isolation
- Tenure is valued more than innovation or well-being
- Leaving is treated as betrayal instead of transition
- Leadership expects gratitude without offering support

Loyalty without boundaries turns into burnout. Staying quiet in the face of chronic dysfunction does not make you a good employee. It makes you vulnerable to emotional erosion.

So how do you reclaim your balance?

1. Redefine Loyalty
Real loyalty includes honesty. It allows room for difficult truths. You can be loyal to your principles and still challenge the practices around you.

2. Set Conditions for Commitment
Ask yourself, "What do I need in return for the energy I give?" Loyalty is not unconditional. It should be based on respect and reciprocity.

3. Separate People from Systems
You can care deeply for coworkers while recognizing that the system they work within is unsustainable. Emotional clarity allows you to navigate both.

4. Permit Yourself to Leave
Leaving is not betrayal. Sometimes it is the most honest response available. Staying too long in a place that does not support your growth benefits no one.

As author and activist Audre Lorde once said, "Caring for myself is not self-indulgence. It is self-preservation, and that is an act of political warfare" (Lorde, 1988).

You do not owe your silence to systems that harm you. You owe yourself honesty, clarity, and protection. That is not disloyal. It is responsible.

True loyalty should not cost you your peace, your voice, or your well-being. ◆

CHAPTER 8

When You've Outgrown the Role

"Workplace stagnation often goes unaddressed because it does not disrupt performance. In fact, it can appear from the outside like everything is going well. You are reliable. You are consistent. You get things done. But inside, you feel like you are shrinking to stay within the box others are comfortable placing you in."

There comes a point in many careers when the role you once felt grateful to have no longer fits. You are still doing the job, possibly even excelling at it, but the learning has stopped. The growth has stalled. The spark is gone.

This shift is not always dramatic. It can begin with subtle boredom, an itch for challenge, or a nagging sense that your talents are being underutilized. You complete your tasks on autopilot. You start to dread meetings that used to energize you. You feel overlooked, even when you are delivering results.

The environment has not necessarily changed. You have.

Workplace stagnation often goes unaddressed because it does not disrupt performance. In fact, it can appear from the outside like everything is going well. You are reliable. You are consistent. You get things done. But inside, you feel like you are shrinking to stay within the box others are comfortable placing you in.

Psychologist Mihaly Csikszentmihalyi, who coined the concept of "flow," emphasized that optimal human experience requires challenge that matches one's skill level. Without it, people fall into states of apathy or frustration (Csikszentmihalyi, 1990). When a job no longer stretches your abilities, it slowly flattens your motivation.

This is not about being entitled or impatient. It is about recognizing that you have evolved, even if your role has not.

Signs you may have outgrown your position include:
- Repeatedly doing the same tasks without learning anything new
- Being praised for consistency but passed over for advancement
- Feeling under-challenged but unsure how to ask for more
- Being discouraged from proposing new ideas
- Watching others be threatened by your initiative

These signs are not failures. They are indicators that you are ready for more.

Unfortunately, some organizations benefit from keeping people in place. Predictability can feel safe to leadership. Promotions may be limited. Growth can be seen as a threat rather than an opportunity. You may be told to "stay in your lane," or praised for being "reliable," while being denied new challenges.

In these moments, it is easy to internalize the limits around you. You begin to question whether you are asking for too much. You wonder if ambition is selfish or if contentment means staying quiet.

But ambition is not arrogance. It is awareness.

You are not disloyal for wanting to expand. You are not ungrateful for recognizing stagnation. You are not a threat for having a vision that extends beyond your current role.

So what can you do?

1. Acknowledge the Shift
Do not minimize it. When you feel your own growth pressing against the boundaries of your role, take it seriously. That discomfort is direction.

2. Get Clear on What You Want
What does growth look like to you? More responsibility? A new skill set? A different kind of impact? Clarity will help guide your next steps.

3. Ask for What You Need
If possible, speak to your manager about expanding responsibilities. Present ideas that align with organizational goals. If the door remains closed, that is data.

4. Document Your Readiness
Track your achievements. Note the ways you have already gone beyond your role. These examples will serve you in future conversations or job searches.

5. Give Yourself Permission to Move On
You are not obligated to stay small to preserve someone else's comfort. Sometimes growth requires changing teams, roles, or organizations altogether.

In *Designing Your Life*, Burnett and Evans write, "You cannot know where you are going until you know where you are" (Burnett & Evans, 2016).

Recognizing that you have outgrown your role is not a problem. It is a starting point.

You do not need to apologize for outgrowing a version of yourself that once fit. You are allowed to stretch. You are allowed to want more. You are allowed to change the shape of your life to match the person you have become. ◆

CHAPTER 9

What Toxic Workplaces Teach You

"Toxic jobs teach you where your limits are. You learn what happens when you ignore them. You become fluent in your own exhaustion and aware of the signals your body sends when something is wrong. Eventually, you start listening."

Toxic work environments often leave scars. They also leave signals, instincts, and insights that stay with you long after you leave. You may not realize it while you are enduring it, but every moment inside that dysfunction was teaching you something. Even when it felt like survival, it was also education.

These lessons are not the ones you signed up for. You probably never intended to become an expert in boundary-setting, emotional detachment, or psychological endurance. Yet somehow, you walked away with a skill set that goes far beyond your job description.

Toxic workplaces teach you how to:

- Spot manipulation dressed up as mentorship
- Recognize gaslighting beneath polite professionalism
- Detect the moment trust leaves a room
- Read between the lines of unclear expectations
- Understand what it feels like to be tolerated instead of valued

This knowledge is not theoretical. It is hard-earned. It is internalized. It becomes part of your radar.

In *The Body Keeps the Score*, psychiatrist Bessel van der Kolk explains how the brain and nervous system adapt to repeated stress and emotional threat. These changes help you survive in unsafe conditions, but they also leave an imprint (van der Kolk, 2014). You become sharper. More discerning. Less tolerant of chaos. You begin to trust what your nervous system picks up before your mind can make sense of it.

Toxic jobs teach you where your limits are. You learn what happens when you ignore them. You become fluent in your own exhaustion and aware of the signals your body sends when something is wrong. Eventually, you start listening.

You learn:

- How to say no without guilt
- That loyalty should never require self-betrayal
- That being liked is not the same as being respected
- That burnout is not proof of dedication
- That peace is not earned through suffering, it is chosen through clarity

Some of the best leaders are shaped by what they had to endure. The ones who have walked through dysfunction often become the most trustworthy. Not because they learned from a manual, but because they remember what it felt like to be treated as expendable. They remember being silenced. They remember what it was like to be invisible, talked over, or dismissed.

They remember the exact moments when they began to shrink.

Those memories become fuel. They build workplaces where others do not have to experience the same harm.

If you are carrying pain from a past job, you are not weak. You are aware.

The anger. The sadness. The guardedness. None of them mean you're broken. They're signals. They point to your values. They remind you of what matters and what you'll never accept again.

In *Rising Strong*, Brené Brown writes, "The irony is that we attempt to disown our difficult stories to appear more whole or more acceptable. But our wholeness — even our wholeheartedness — actually depends on the integration of all our experiences, including the falls" (Brown, 2015).

You are allowed to carry the wisdom without carrying the weight. You are allowed to use your pain as data, not identity. You are allowed to outgrow the version of yourself who had to endure that job.

Toxic workplaces do not just teach you how to endure. They teach you how to rebuild. ◆

CHAPTER 10

How to Cope
When You Can't Care Anymore

"There comes a point when the effort to care becomes too expensive. You stop raising your hand in meetings. You stop offering feedback. You stop trying to solve problems no one listens to. At first, you care too much. Then you care just enough. Eventually, you do not care at all."

There comes a point when the effort to care becomes too expensive. You stop raising your hand in meetings. You stop offering feedback. You stop trying to solve problems no one listens to. At first, you care too much. Then you care just enough. Eventually, you do not care at all.

This shift is not laziness. It is a form of emotional self-preservation. Psychologists refer to it as disengagement, and it often follows prolonged exposure to chronic stress or environments where your voice does not matter. The longer you try without seeing change, the harder it becomes to keep trying.

Gallup's 2023 *Global Workplace Report* found that 59 percent of workers are "quiet quitting." This term describes employees who fulfill their job requirements but stop going above and beyond. It is not a rebellion. It is often a last attempt to conserve energy in a system that rewards overwork and under-appreciation.

Disengagement does not always look like withdrawal. Sometimes it looks like:

- Nodding politely in meetings without internal agreement
- Avoiding eye contact with management
- Completing tasks with zero emotional investment
- Feeling relief when meetings are canceled
- Avoiding conflict because nothing changes anyway

This version of coping may keep the peace externally, but internally, it leaves people feeling empty.

Burnout is defined as a syndrome resulting from chronic workplace stress that has not been successfully managed. It is characterized by exhaustion, mental distance from one's job, and reduced professional efficacy (World Health Organization, 2019). Once you hit this point, caring feels dangerous. It feels like the faster route to depletion.

If this is where you find yourself, you are not alone. You are not broken. You are tired of giving more than you get.

Here are a few ways to stabilize your emotional footing when caring has become too costly:

1. Acknowledge the shift.
Pretending you still care at the same level does not protect you.

It disconnects you. Be honest with yourself about what has changed. That is where clarity begins.

2. Detach without numbing.
It is possible to emotionally detach from outcomes without becoming cynical. You can hold boundaries while maintaining integrity. Detachment is not coldness. It is self-respect.

3. Redefine what care looks like.
Sometimes care is staying quiet to protect your peace. Sometimes it is walking away from fights that go nowhere. Caring differently is still caring.

4. Stop trying to rescue systems.
You are not responsible for fixing what leadership will not address. You can care about your work without carrying the dysfunction.

5. Shift your energy toward what is next.
If your current role cannot meet you with respect or recognition, begin building the bridge to your next opportunity. The sooner you channel your energy forward, the less stuck you will feel.

This chapter is not about convincing you to care again. It is about validating why you stopped. It is about honoring the fatigue that comes with emotional labor and misplaced hope.

In *Emotional Agility*, psychologist Susan David wrote, "Discomfort is the price of admission to a meaningful life" (David, 2016).

Choosing to care again, even selectively, takes courage. But it does not need to happen all at once. The goal is not to become the perfect employee. The goal is to become a healthier version of yourself, even in environments that did not deserve your full care.

You may not care the way you used to. That does not mean you no longer care at all. It means you have learned to survive by conserving the most precious thing you have: your energy. ◆

CHAPTER 11

When You're Good at the Work
but Miserable in the Role

"This is not about capability. It is about capacity. You can be competent and still feel depleted. You can do excellent work in an environment that chips away at your well-being."

It is a strange kind of pain to be good at your job and still dread showing up. You meet deadlines, exceed expectations, and maybe even receive praise. From the outside, everything looks fine. Internally, you are unraveling.

This is not about capability. It is about capacity. You can be competent and still feel depleted. You can do excellent work in an environment that chips away at your well-being.

Many people stay in roles longer than they should because they are told their performance means they should be happy. If you are succeeding, what could possibly be wrong? The answer is simple: performance does not equal fulfillment.

People are not driven solely by external rewards like money or praise. Instead, they crave autonomy, mastery, and purpose. If your job stifles these elements, even the best compensation package will not make up for the disconnect (Pink, 2009).

Here is what that disconnect often sounds like:

- "I know I should be grateful, but I feel numb."
- "I am good at what I do, but I do not feel seen."
- "I do everything right, but it still feels wrong."
- "I am praised for results, not for being a person."

These are not complaints. They are signals. Signals that something deeper is missing.

Sometimes the issue is the environment: a toxic culture, an absent leader, or a lack of support. Other times it is misalignment between your values and your employer's, or between your talents and what the role actually demands.

When you are skilled at what you do, people often assume you are thriving. You may even use your success as proof that you should stay. But if the work is draining your mental or emotional health, no amount of praise can make it sustainable.

Here are four truths to hold onto when you feel stuck between success and misery:

1. Being good at something does not mean you owe it your peace.
Just because you can tolerate something does not mean you should. Excellence without well-being is a short-term equation.

2. Praise is not the same as purpose.
Recognition feels good. But it cannot replace meaning. If you are being celebrated for work that does not reflect your values, the applause will eventually ring hollow.

3. Staying for validation will only deepen the disconnection.
If you stay just to prove you are valuable, you may lose sight of your actual value. You do not have to keep earning approval you already deserve.

4. Misery is not a requirement for mastery.
You do not have to suffer to grow. Challenge can be healthy. But chronic dissatisfaction is not a badge of honor. It is a warning.

In *The War of Art*, Steven Pressfield wrote, "Resistance will tell you anything to keep you from doing your work. It will perjure, fabricate; it will seduce you. Resistance is insidious" (Pressfield, 2002).

Sometimes that resistance shows up as comfort. It tells you to stay where you are because you are good at it. It tells you to settle because others have it worse. But survival is not the goal. Alignment is.

You can be grateful for your skills while still longing for something better. You can take pride in what you have built without staying in a role that no longer fits. Being good at the work is not a reason to ignore how you feel.

Misery is not the price of success. You are allowed to want more, even when you are already performing well. ◆

CHAPTER 12

The Trap of Being the "Strong One" at Work

"Being the "strong one" at work means people come to you for answers, lean on you during chaos, and expect you to absorb stress without complaint. Over time, this creates an environment where your needs are overlooked simply because you never voice them."

There is an unspoken pressure placed on the person who appears the most capable. If you handle pressure well, meet every deadline, and never visibly crack, you become the one everyone relies on. That reputation can feel like both a compliment and a trap.

Being the "strong one" at work means people come to you for answers, lean on you during chaos, and expect you to absorb stress without complaint. Over time, this creates an environment where your needs are overlooked simply because you never voice them.

This role often begins subtly. You take on a few extra tasks to support the team. You say yes when you would rather say no. You stay late because no one else will. Eventually, this becomes expected instead of appreciated. What was once generosity turns into obligation.

Research in occupational health psychology shows that role overload and emotional labor disproportionately affect high-performing employees, particularly those who feel responsible for team cohesion. According to a study published in the *Journal of Applied Psychology*, employees who internalize the role of "the dependable one" are significantly more prone to burnout, presenteeism, and emotional exhaustion (Gabriel, Koopman, Rosen, & Johnson, 2021).

The pressure to remain composed at all times becomes isolating. If you show emotion, people are surprised. If you express frustration, they assume something is seriously wrong. The moment you ask for help, it feels like a disruption to the status quo.

The longer you maintain the image of invincibility, the harder it becomes to break it. Vulnerability feels risky. Rest feels undeserved. Asking for support feels like weakness, even though it is not.

Here are five truths for anyone who has become the unofficial emotional support system at work:

1. Strength does not require silence.
Being strong is not about absorbing everything. It is about knowing when to speak up. Silence may keep the peace temporarily, but often at the cost of your well-being.

2. Boundaries are not betrayal.
Saying no does not make you selfish. It makes you sustainable. Boundaries are not walls. They are doors that protect what matters.

3. Support should be mutual.

If you are always the one giving but rarely receiving, the relationship is out of balance. Even in professional environments, reciprocity is a form of respect.

4. You do not need to earn your worth through sacrifice.

Your value does not increase with exhaustion. Being consistently overextended is not a badge of honor. It is a warning sign.

5. Vulnerability is not weakness. It is truth.

"Vulnerability is not winning or losing. It is having the courage to show up and be seen when we have no control over the outcome" (Brown, 2012, p. 2). Letting others see you when you are tired, overwhelmed, or unsure is not a failure of strength. It is evidence of being human.

You can be reliable and still need rest. You can lead others and still need support. You can care deeply and still reach a limit. These truths can coexist.

The next time you feel compelled to prove your strength by staying silent or saying yes when you mean no, pause. Ask yourself if strength in this moment means pushing through or stepping back.

The goal is not to stop being dependable. The goal is to stop equating self-sacrifice with value.

You are not a machine. You are a person. Even the strong ones deserve space to breathe. ◆

CHAPTER 13

When Feedback Feels Like Failure

"In high-pressure or psychologically unsafe workplaces, feedback is rarely neutral. It becomes a test of loyalty, a performance review disguised as casual input, or a strategic way to reassert hierarchy. It feels less like guidance and more like a warning."

Feedback is supposed to help us grow. Constructive criticism, when delivered with care and clarity, can sharpen our skills and build confidence. But in many workplaces, feedback does not feel constructive. It feels personal. It feels like failure.

The problem is not always the feedback itself. It is how, when, and why it is delivered. Vague feedback without context. Criticism offered only during review season. Performance conversations framed as personality flaws. Over time, this does not build resilience. It creates shame.

According to psychologist Carol Dweck's research on mindset, people respond to evaluation based on their internal beliefs. Those with a growth mindset view feedback as a path to improvement. Those operating under fear or chronic stress interpret feedback as evidence of inadequacy. The same comment can land entirely differently depending on the environment in which it is received (Dweck, 2006).

In high-pressure or psychologically unsafe workplaces, feedback is rarely neutral. It becomes a test of loyalty, a performance review disguised as casual input, or a strategic way to reassert hierarchy. It feels less like guidance and more like a warning.

The emotional toll shows up in familiar ways:

- Bracing yourself every time someone says, "Can I give you some feedback?"
- Ruminating for hours after a single sentence of critique
- Assuming you are in trouble even when you are not
- Feeling unseen for everything you did well, and targeted for what you missed

This dynamic is especially damaging in workplaces that praise effort publicly but critique privately. Employees begin to mistrust praise because they know a reprimand often follows. Inconsistency becomes the culture.

Psychological safety is the belief that you will not be punished or humiliated for speaking up with ideas, questions, or mistakes (Edmondson, 2019).

In a psychologically safe workplace, feedback becomes a tool for alignment, not shame. But when that safety is missing, feedback becomes emotionally loaded. Even well-intentioned input can feel like an attack.

To navigate this, it helps to shift your internal relationship with feedback:

1. Consider the source.
Ask yourself: is this person invested in your growth, or simply asserting power? Not all feedback deserves your full emotional response.

2. Separate content from tone.
A poorly delivered message can still contain helpful truth. Pull out the part that serves you and leave the rest.

3. Keep a record of positive feedback.
Create a "praise file" with emails, notes, or compliments you have received. When criticism lands hard, remind yourself of your full track record.

4. Normalize feedback as data.
Feedback is not a moral judgment. It is one perspective. You are allowed to disagree. You are also allowed to grow without internalizing shame.

"Becoming is better than being." (Mindset, Dweck, 2006, p. 17). The goal is not perfection. It is evolution.

If feedback has become a source of fear instead of growth, it is not your fault. You may be receiving it in a culture that confuses correction with control. You still have power. That power is in how you process, respond, and move forward.

You are not failing just because someone found a flaw. You are finally evolving. ◆

CHAPTER 14

When Your Job Becomes Your Identity

*"There is a difference between doing meaningful
work and needing work to define your meaning."*

There is a difference between doing meaningful work and needing work to define your meaning. In a culture that rewards overachievement, it is easy to lose track of where the job ends, and the person begins.

This is especially common in high-responsibility roles. You are praised for going above and beyond. You are trusted because you always deliver. Eventually, your value gets measured by your output. Praise reinforces performance. Quiet quitting feels like moral failure. Over time, you start introducing yourself as what you do, not who you are.

A rising trend of identity entanglement with work has been observed, particularly in high-burnout professions. The more personal fulfillment is tied to professional performance, the more emotionally devastating it feels when things begin to unravel. A toxic job then becomes more than a bad experience; it becomes a perceived reflection of self-worth (American Psychological Association, 2022).

The difference between internal self-awareness (how clearly we see ourselves) and external self-awareness (how we think others see us) is significant. In many workplace environments, external perception dominates. We measure our worth based on performance reviews, productivity metrics, or managerial approval (Eurich, 2018).

When your job becomes your identity, certain signs begin to show:

- Your mood rises or falls based on feedback from your boss
- You feel anxious during downtime or vacation because you are not being productive
- You struggle to describe yourself without mentioning your job title
- You feel personally attacked when work is criticized, even when it is not about you

None of this means you are weak. It means you have spent years in a system that taught you to equate success with identity. In many cases, it was not a conscious choice. It was survival.

But survival mode is not meant to last forever.

"You either walk inside your story and own it, or you stand outside your story and hustle for your worthiness" (Brown, 2010, p. 23). Reclaiming your identity from your job begins with walking back into your own story. Not the version built around performance or praise, but the version rooted in your full humanity.

Here are a few ways to start separating your sense of self from your workplace role:

1. Revisit what you loved before work took over.
Return to hobbies or interests that have nothing to do with productivity. These activities are not frivolous. They are reminders of your full identity.

2. Set boundaries that protect your time.
You are not being selfish by ending the workday on time. You are being responsible for your long-term well-being.

3. Practice describing yourself without titles.
Try this: "I'm someone who values creativity and connection," instead of "I'm a project manager." Shift how you view yourself, and the world often responds differently.

4. Find communities outside your profession.
Your value expands when your environment does. Spend time around people who care about who you are, not just what you achieve.

Work can be part of your identity. It just should not be the whole thing.

You are more than your role. More than your output. More than what someone else thinks of your performance.

There is a version of you beyond the burnout. You do not have to earn the right to be that person. ◆

CHAPTER 15

What You Take With You

"Toxic jobs often function as an unexpected kind of training. Unfair, exhausting, and emotionally draining, but training nonetheless. You learn to spot subtle power plays. You learn how it feels to be talked over, underestimated, or misjudged. You also learn how to trust your gut and build emotional armor without losing your core self."

Leaving a toxic job does not mean you walk away empty-handed. In fact, you take more with you than you may realize.

You take sharper instincts, stronger boundaries, and a refined radar for dysfunction. You take the clarity that comes from knowing what you will never allow again. You carry the internal proof that you showed up even when it would have been easier to give up.

Toxic jobs often function as an unexpected kind of training. Unfair, exhausting, and emotionally draining, but training nonetheless. You learn to spot subtle power plays. You learn how it feels to be talked over, underestimated, or misjudged. You also learn how to trust your gut and build emotional armor without losing your core self.

This growth is real. It may not look like a promotion or a title change, but it changes you.

Harvard Business Review notes that employees who leave high-stress, high-conflict environments often become stronger leaders because they know how poor leadership feels from the inside (Coutu, 2002). These individuals tend to lead with empathy, recognize emotional cues more quickly, and hold clearer boundaries.

You also bring with you your quiet victories. These are the small but significant moments when you upheld your values. The times you remained calm in chaos.

The days you helped teammates without recognition. The ways you protected others even when no one protected you.

In her book *The Gift*, Dr. Edith Eger writes, "Our painful experiences aren't a liability; they're a gift. They give us perspective and meaning, an opportunity to find our unique purpose and our strength" (Eger, 2020, p. 24). You are not walking away empty. You are walking away wiser.

You now know what emotional manipulation looks like. You know how it feels to be left out, talked over, or set up to fail. You also know how to see through fake encouragement and performative praise. That is not bitterness. That is experience.

You leave with more than wounds. You leave with wisdom.

Even if that job tried to convince you otherwise, your value never left you. It was buried under the weight of dysfunction. But it was always there.

You are not the same person who walked in on day one. That person might have been more trusting or more eager to prove themselves. The person who walks out is more aware, more grounded, and far more equipped to protect what matters.

You did not waste your time. You earned insight the hard way. And now, it is yours to use. ◆

CHAPTER 16

You Deserve to Enjoy Work

"Enjoying work is not about perks, office snacks, or a boss who remembers your birthday. It is about feeling psychologically safe enough to bring your full self. It is about being valued not only for your output but also for your insight. It is about being in a space that does not drain your spirit in the name of productivity."

You did not come this far just to survive. You came this far to evolve.

Liking your work, or even simply not dreading it, is not asking too much. It is asking for what most people were led to expect: that effort, talent, and consistency would lead to meaning, progress, and stability.

That promise does not always appear in the form we imagined. Still, it is not out of reach. You may need to define it for yourself, based on your values instead of someone else's.

Enjoying work is not about perks, office snacks, or a boss who remembers your birthday. It is about feeling psychologically safe enough to bring your full self. It is about being valued not only for your output but also for your insight. It is about being in a space that does not drain your spirit in the name of productivity.

You may not get to choose every role you take. You always get to choose how you show up in it. You can decide how to recover, how to rebuild, and how to determine what comes next. You can also choose what you will no longer tolerate and which version of yourself you are willing to bring forward.

Enjoyment is not a luxury. It is a signal that your dignity, your energy, and your humanity are intact. When those are protected, even in small ways, your entire relationship with work begins to shift.

If you feel stuck, begin with the smallest signs of life. Look for moments of progress, people who affirm you, laughter that feels real, or work that sparks curiosity. These fragments of connection are not trivial. They are indicators of what you need more of.

The goal is not just to survive your job. The goal is to outgrow what hurt you and build something more aligned.

In *Drive: The Surprising Truth About What Motivates Us*, author Daniel H. Pink explains that true engagement at work is rooted in autonomy, mastery, and purpose. It does not come from compliance or fear (Pink, 2009). When those three elements are present, people thrive. When they are absent, people disengage.

You deserve to work in an environment where those qualities are nurtured. If that is not your current reality, it is still something to move toward.

Your past experiences may have shaped you, but they do not define you. You are allowed to want more. You are allowed to believe it is possible. You are allowed to build it on your terms. ◆

CHAPTER 17

Why Toxic Jobs Stay With You

"A toxic job can shape your wiring. But it does not get to shape your future. You get to choose how much power it continues to hold."

Leaving a toxic job may offer relief, but it rarely brings instant peace. The effects linger. Long after you submit your resignation, certain habits, fears, and mental patterns follow you into new roles.

This is not a sign that you are weak. It is a natural consequence of prolonged exposure to environments that distort your sense of safety and self-worth.

The body and mind adapt to survive. Over time, you may have learned to downplay your needs, anticipate criticism, or scan every conversation for hidden meaning. These behaviors do not automatically disappear once the job ends. They become embedded in your nervous system.

According to Dr. Bessel van der Kolk in *The Body Keeps the Score*, traumatic stress reshapes both brain function and emotional regulation. Work-related trauma, while often minimized, can leave similar imprints. People may develop hyper-vigilance, struggle with trust, or experience anxiety in otherwise healthy environments (van der Kolk, 2014).

This does not mean you are broken. It means your brain did its job. It learned how to protect you under pressure.

Healing from that kind of environment takes intention. You must unlearn patterns that once kept you safe but now hold you back.

Common lingering effects include:

- Over-apologizing for small things
- Difficulty accepting praise or recognition
- Anxiety around authority figures
- Fear of taking initiative or asking questions
- Constantly preparing for something to go wrong

These habits are not personality flaws. They are survival mechanisms. With time, they can be softened and replaced.

Healing begins with recognition. It is the process of noticing where the past is still running the present. From there, you can start to rebuild trust in yourself and in healthier systems.

Here are steps that can help:

1. Name what happened.
Use accurate language. If you experienced gaslighting, manipulation,

or harassment, call it what it was. Naming creates clarity and breaks internal confusion.

2. Affirm your reality.
Your exhaustion, self-doubt, or hesitation did not come from nowhere. They were earned responses. Treat them with compassion.

3. Find safe environments.
Whether in work, friendship, or therapy, prioritize spaces where your voice is heard and your experience is believed.

4. Track your growth.
Keep record of the moments you spoke up, held a boundary, or trusted your instincts. Healing is rarely linear, but progress is worth documenting.

Dr. Therma Bryant writes in *Homecoming* that healing requires "unlearning what we were taught to believe about ourselves when we were in survival mode" (Bryant, 2022, p. 19). Recovery does not erase what happened. It reclaims your sense of self.

A toxic job can shape your wiring. But it does not get to shape your future. You get to choose how much power it continues to hold.

Each step you take toward healing is an act of quiet resistance. Each moment of peace is proof that you are no longer stuck in survival. ◆

CHAPTER 18

What Healing Actually Looks Like

"Self-trust is often the first casualty of a toxic environment. Rebuilding that trust takes time. It begins when you learn to listen to yourself again."

Healing from a toxic work experience is not always dramatic or visible. Sometimes it looks like crying on your lunch break and still showing up the next day. Sometimes it looks like pausing before you apologize unnecessarily. Sometimes it is the quiet decision to stop internalizing every piece of criticism.

The truth is that healing rarely looks like triumph. It often looks like subtle shifts, small wins, and choosing not to abandon yourself, even when the world taught you to.

There is no single path to recovery. Healing is not linear. Emotional recovery from workplace trauma depends on several factors, including perceived support, self-awareness, and access to psychological resources (American Psychological Association, 2023). Progress may come slowly, but it still counts.

Healing may show up as:

- Speaking up in a meeting without rehearsing your words
- Noticing tension in your body and choosing to rest instead of push through
- Replacing self-blame with curiosity when something goes wrong
- Letting go of perfectionism long enough to breathe

It is easy to overlook these moments. They do not get celebrated. They are not listed on performance reviews. Yet they are some of the most important acts of growth a person can make.

Self-trust is often the first casualty of a toxic environment. Rebuilding that trust takes time. It begins when you learn to listen to yourself again.

You might still hear the voice of your old boss in your head when you hesitate. You might still brace for backlash when giving feedback. These echoes do not mean you have failed to move on. They are reminders of how deeply conditioned your nervous system became.

Dr. Gabor Maté, in *The Myth of Normal*, reminds us that trauma is not what happens to you, but what happens inside you as a result of what happened. Healing, then, is the process of making yourself safe inside your own body again (Maté & Maté, 2022).

It does not happen overnight. But it does happen.

Here are reminders to yourself:

1. You are not behind.
There is no universal timeline for recovery. Your pace is valid.

2. You are allowed to feel joy again.
Healing includes laughter, rest, and moments of peace. You do not have to earn those.

3. You can hold both anger and grace.
You can be furious at what happened and still show yourself compassion.

4. You are not defined by how long you stayed.
You are defined by what you learned and how you choose to move forward.

Healing from a toxic job is real work. It requires patience, self-reflection, and often grief. It also creates a new foundation, one that is built not on fear, but on clarity.

You may not have chosen what happened to you. But you get to choose what happens next. ◆

CHAPTER 19

How to Rebuild
Without Losing Yourself

*"Rebuilding after a toxic job is not just about updating your résumé.
It is about restoring trust in your judgment, instincts, and ability to
thrive in a healthier environment."*

After leaving a toxic job, many people experience a strange kind of disorientation. The chaos is gone, but so is the structure. The pressure has lifted but so has the sense of direction. You are free, but unsure of who you are now that the fight is over.

This is a normal phase of recovery.

Every major life transition involves three stages: an ending, a neutral zone, and a new beginning. The neutral zone, the space between what was and what comes next, can feel like limbo, but it is also where renewal begins (Bridges, 2004).

Rebuilding after a toxic job is not just about updating your résumé. It is about restoring trust in your judgment, instincts, and ability to thrive in a healthier environment.

You may second-guess everything at first. You may worry that you are carrying too much emotional weight into your next chapter. That is not a sign of weakness. It is a sign that you are trying to move forward with intention.

Here is what rebuilding can include:

1. Redefining success on your terms
Ask yourself what success feels like, not just what it looks like. Is it peace? Is it autonomy? Is it respect? Let those answers guide your next move.

2. Noticing your nervous system
If you flinch when someone schedules a meeting or feel anxious at the sound of a notification, your body may still be responding to past conditions. Healing begins when you notice those responses without judgment and learn to meet them with care.

3. Being selective
You do not owe every organization your time or talent. You are allowed to assess their culture, leadership, and alignment with your values. Interviews now go both ways.

4. Choosing a human pace, you are not a machine
You do not have to rebound immediately. You are allowed to recover slowly, thoughtfully, and in a way that honors your well-being.

Rebuilding is not just about finding a job. It is about reclaiming your story and shifting it from one of survival to one of strength. "Owning our story and loving ourselves through that process is the bravest thing we'll ever do" (Brown, 2010, p. 17).

You are not starting over. You are starting from experience.

This version of you is more aware. You are no longer easily impressed by vague promises or surface-level culture claims. You are clearer about your boundaries and more confident in your ability to protect them.

There is no deadline for healing. The fact that you made it out is already proof of your strength. ◆

CHAPTER 20

Building a New Vision for Work

"A new vision of work is not built from fantasy. It is constructed through reflection, clarity, and intentional decision-making."

Once you have left the damage behind, the next question becomes, "What do I want my work life to feel like?"

This is not always easy to answer. When someone has spent years in survival mode, it can be difficult to imagine anything beyond exhaustion. However, healing does not stop at recovery. It continues with redesign. The goal is not only to avoid what harmed you. The goal is to pursue something better.

A new vision of work is not built from fantasy. It is constructed through reflection, clarity, and intentional decision-making. It asks you to reimagine the role work plays in your life and how that relationship can support, not sabotage, your well-being.

Here are the foundational elements of a healthier vision:

1. Alignment Over Approval

In toxic workplaces, many people learn to contort themselves for approval. In healthier environments, alignment becomes more important. Ask yourself: Does this role support who I am becoming? Do the values, communication style, and leadership philosophy align with how I want to live?

2. Boundaries That Stick

A new vision of work cannot exist without boundaries. This includes not checking emails at midnight, not attending meetings that serve no purpose, and not absorbing emotional labor that does not belong to you. These limits are not selfish. They are structural. They allow you to stay functional, clear-headed, and present.

3. Purpose That Feels Real

Seventy percent of employees say their sense of purpose is defined by their work (Chow, Heller, & Stewart, 2022). If your job does not align with your values, disconnection is inevitable. Whether your purpose is about helping people, creating solutions, or solving problems, your work should reflect at least part of that drive.

4. Psychological Safety

Workplaces that lack safety drive silence, fear, and burnout. Psychological safety s defined as "a belief that one will not be punished or humiliated for speaking up with ideas, questions, concerns, or mistakes" (Edmondson, 1999). Without it, creativity dies. With it, trust and innovation thrive.

5. Sustainable Growth

You do not need rapid advancement or endless titles to feel successful. You need room to grow at a pace that respects your mental and physical health. Healthy work environments provide challenge without exploitation. They encourage learning without punishment.

A new vision does not have to be perfect. It just has to be honest. Maybe you want to work for a smaller team. Maybe you want to work remotely. Maybe you want fewer meetings, more deep work time, or the freedom to bring your whole personality to your role. The details matter less than the self-awareness that leads you to them.

Designing a better work life also means recognizing your patterns. If you have a tendency to over function, take on too much, or derive worth from being needed, these traits will follow you unless addressed. A new job is not a new identity. You bring yourself with you. Make sure that version is one you are proud to carry.

Healing from a toxic workplace is not the end of the story. It is the beginning of something more deliberate. You deserve work that supports your values, not just your bills. You deserve peace, not just productivity.

Work will never be perfect. But it can become a place where you no longer lose yourself. ◆

CHAPTER 21

Staying Free After You Leave

"Leaving the job was only the beginning. The next challenge is staying free from the habits, beliefs, and fears that kept you stuck for so long."

Leaving the job was only the beginning. The next challenge is staying free from the habits, beliefs, and fears that kept you stuck for so long.

It is easy to walk away physically while still carrying the emotional residue. Toxic environments have a way of embedding themselves in your nervous system. Long after the exit interview, you might still flinch at emails, over-apologize in meetings, or doubt your own judgment. That is not weakness. That is conditioning.

Recovery means doing more than surviving. It means choosing not to replicate the dynamics that once harmed you.

Here are five reminders to help protect your freedom as you move forward:

1. Stop Explaining Yourself to People Who Don't Listen
Not everyone deserves an explanation. If someone continually dismisses your experience or minimizes your boundaries, their confusion is not your responsibility. Clarifying your values does not require audience approval.

2. Notice When You're Playing Small
Sometimes freedom looks like speaking up again. Other times, it looks like taking a risk, applying for the role, or raising your rate. If you shrink yourself out of habit, it is time to recalibrate.

3. Separate Feedback from Truth
Feedback is information, not identity. Just because a former boss questioned your competence does not make it a fact. Use discernment. Ask whether the feedback was accurate, helpful, or just a projection of someone else's insecurity.

4. Let Rest Become Normal
Burnout culture teaches people to equate worth with output. That mindset is hard to unlearn. But sustainable work requires recovery. Normalize quiet weekends, full lunch breaks, and shutting your laptop without guilt.

The World Health Organization formally classified burnout as an occupational phenomenon in 2019. It is not laziness. It is a state of chronic workplace stress that has not been successfully managed (World Health Organization, 2019). Rest is not indulgence. It is repair.

5. Choose Self-Trust Over Fear

In trauma-informed coaching, there is a principle called "post-traumatic growth." It refers to the positive psychological change that occurs as a result of struggle (Tedeschi & Calhoun, 2004). You went through something difficult, and you learned from it. Do not let fear drag you backward. Use that wisdom to lead yourself forward.

The real win is not just that you left. It is that you are learning to live differently afterward.

You are building a work life that honors your needs, not just your resume. You are learning to trust your inner voice again. You are giving yourself permission to rebuild, not with urgency, but with intention.

Freedom is not a single decision. It is a daily practice. ◆

CHAPTER 22

Redefining Success on Your Terms

"One of the quietest, most radical things you can do after leaving a harmful job is redefine what success means to you."

One of the quietest, most radical things you can do after leaving a harmful job is redefine what success means to you.

Most people are handed a definition early in life. Success means promotions, bigger titles, higher paychecks, and external validation. These markers are often designed by industries that benefit from constant striving. They rarely reflect joy, balance, or personal growth.

When you leave a toxic workplace, you may experience a strange sense of emptiness. Not because you want to go back, but because you are unsure what to aim for now.

This is your invitation to redefine success based on your values, not outdated metrics.

1. Ask What You Want, Not Just What You Want to Escape
It is easy to say you do not want micromanagement, chaos, or burnout. The harder question is what you want instead. Do you want freedom? Trust? A sense of meaning? Begin with what lights you up, not just what used to dim you.

2. Use Internal Goals as Your Compass
Psychologists have found that intrinsic goals such as personal growth, meaningful relationships, and community contribution lead to greater well-being than extrinsic goals like fame or wealth (Deci & Ryan, 2000). When you prioritize internal rewards, you protect your mental health and autonomy.

3. Let Progress Look Different Now
Success might look like not checking your email after 6 p.m. It might look like setting boundaries or turning down work that does not align with your values. These moments may seem small, but they build a new foundation. You are not behind. You are rebuilding.

4. Release the Need to Constantly Prove Yourself
Many high achievers in toxic environments develop a hyper-vigilant work style. Even after leaving, they feel the need to earn rest, justify downtime, or outperform their peers. This is residue, not reality. Letting go of this mindset is not lazy. It is healthy.

5. Choose Alignment Over Approval
Real success is often quiet. It does not always look impressive on LinkedIn. But when your values match your actions, you create internal

peace. That peace is worth more than any title.

"Authenticity is a collection of choices that we have to make every day. It is about the choice to show up and be real" (Brown, 2010, p. 49). Real success starts there.

You are allowed to want a life that feels good, not just one that looks good. You are allowed to outgrow old goals and define new ones based on who you are now, not who you were when you entered that last job.

Success that costs your health, joy, or sense of self is not success. It is sacrifice.

You did not leave one difficult chapter just to write another with the same rules.

You get to build a new story now. ◆

CHAPTER 23

Reclaiming Your Power at Work

"Choosing presence over fear, action over silence, and boundaries over burnout is where real power begins. There is no need to overpower anyone. The shift begins when you stop abandoning yourself."

After working in an environment that made you feel small, invisible, or replaceable, reclaiming your sense of power can feel unfamiliar. This is not because you lack power, but because the environment conditioned you to forget it. Workplaces built on control or fear often erode self-trust. People begin to question their instincts, silence their voices, and measure their worth by how well they avoid conflict.

Over time, it can seem as though power only belongs to others. Authentic power is not about dominance. It is about agency. It is the ability to act in alignment with your values. It is the quiet strength to speak clearly, even when it is uncomfortable. It is the choice to protect your dignity rather than abandon it.

Begin with Awareness

Reclaiming power begins with noticing where it has been handed away. These are moments when credit is avoided, silence is chosen instead of clarity, or personal limits are ignored to meet external expectations. These actions may seem minor, but they slowly reshape self-perception.

Boundaries Are Not Selfish

"Setting boundaries is not rejection. It is preservation. Boundaries protect what is important to you" (Tawwab, 2021). They are not meant to push others away, but to keep you intact.

Rebuild Self-Trust

Toxic workplaces often encourage people to defer to others, even when doing so contradicts their values. Trusting your instincts is essential. Your emotional and mental responses are not flaws. They are feedback. You are allowed to believe your own experience.

Use Direct, Respectful Language

Communication reinforces identity. When you speak, choose words that reflect certainty and calm. Say, "I need more information," instead of, "Sorry, I just have a question." Assertiveness does not require aggression. It requires clarity.

Surround Yourself with Supportive People

The people around you influence how you see yourself. Community is not optional. It is critical. Find spaces where your voice is heard, your values are shared, and your strengths are recognized.

Power exists in how you carry yourself, how you respond to pressure, and how you protect what matters. It is not assigned by rank or job title.

It is reclaimed through conscious effort and daily choices.

"Realize deeply that the present moment is all you ever have. Make the Now the primary focus of your life" (Tolle, 1997, p. 40). This includes how you show up in your work life.

Choosing presence over fear, action over silence, and boundaries over burnout is where real power begins. There is no need to overpower anyone. The shift begins when you stop abandoning yourself. ◆

WORKBOOK

Your Personal Power Workbook

A 7-Page Tool To Reclaim
Your Energy, Voice, and Direction at Work

HOW TO USE THIS WORKBOOK

This isn't about overthinking. It's about clarity. Treat it like a tool, not a journal. Use it to pinpoint what's draining you, what you're tolerating, and what needs to change. It's direct on purpose. Skip what doesn't apply. Focus on what does. Do the pages that make you uncomfortable. That's where the shift starts.

My Intention for This Workbook:

_____
_____
_____
_____
_____
_____
_____
_____
_____
_____
_____
_____
_____
_____
_____
_____
_____
_____
_____
_____
_____
_____
_____
_____
_____

Your Reality Check
No filters. No fluff. Just facts.

What do I complain about the most?

_____

_____

_____

_____

_____

Who or what consistently wears me down?

_____

_____

_____

_____

_____

Where have I given up control?

_____

_____

_____

_____

_____

Energy Check
Rate your days (1=drained, 5=solid):

Mon: __ | Tue: __ | Wed: __ | Thu: __ | Fri: __

What gave you a little boost?

_____

_____

_____

_____

What dragged you down?

_____

_____

_____

_____

Real Problems, Practical Moves

You don't need inspiration. You need direction. Pick the ones that land. Then take action.

If you're getting ignored or passed over:
- Drop the disclaimers. Say what needs to be said.
- Track what you've done. Call it out clearly. No softening.

_____

_____

_____

_____

_____

_____

_____

If you keep second-guessing yourself:
- Write down one time your gut was dead-on. What did it feel like?
- Decide now what you'll do the next time that same feeling shows up.

_____

_____

_____

_____

_____

_____

_____

If you're saying yes too much:
- Pick one thing you're done doing. Say no. Mean it.
- Script your response ahead of time. Use it. No apologies.

_____

_____

_____

_____

_____

_____

_____

If you've been avoiding hard conversations:
- Write the sentence you've been sidestepping.
- Say it. Don't wait for the right time. Just be clear.

_____

_____

_____

_____

_____

_____

_____

If work feels meaningless lately:
- Name your top 3 values. Apply one this week — in real terms.
- Define what success looks like to you. Not anyone else.

_____

_____

_____

_____

_____

_____

_____

Boundaries You Actually Keep
Top 3 Non-Negotiable's:

Boundary 1: _____

Why it matters: _____

How I'll hold It: _____

_____

_____

_____

Boundary 2: _____

Why it matters: _____

How I'll hold It: _____

_____

_____

_____

Boundary 3: _____

Why it matters: _____

How I'll hold It: _____

_____

_____

_____

Who's Actually in My Corner

_____has my back because:_____
_____has my back because:_____
_____has my back because:_____

Who gives it to me straight when I need it?

_____

_____

_____

_____

What colleagues, friends or community sharpens me, not drains me?

_____

_____

_____

_____

Three ways I'll keep these ties strong:

1. _____

_____

_____

2. _____

_____

_____

3. _____

_____

_____

What Comes Next

Three things I'll act on this month:

1. _____

_____

_____

_____

_____

2. _____

_____

_____

_____

_____

3. _____

_____

_____

_____

_____

How I'll track my progress (not perfection - just proof):

_____

_____

_____

MESSAGE TO EMPLOYERS, MANAGERS, & LEADERS

If you lead people, hire people, or influence the way people experience work, this is for you.

This book was written for those who once felt clear, capable, and fully invested in their work. Over time, they began to carry the weight of a culture that made it harder to keep showing up.

After all, if you truly noticed, you would have fixed it. No leader with integrity lets their team continue to struggle when the cause is clear and correctable. Choosing not to act makes you part of the problem. Not all workplace issues are the same. I understand that. Some people bring bad attitudes, entitlement, or emotional instability into the mix. But it is still your responsibility to create an environment where everyone has the opportunity to flourish, if they choose.

Problem employees can erode progress, morale, and the trust of a good team. This is not easy, but it is critical. You have to assess it often and handle it directly. Avoiding it only drags everyone down.

If this hit a nerve, it is not by accident. It is showing you exactly where to look.

If this offends you, you are likely part of the problem. If it informs you, you are part of the solution.

There is no neutral ground. Every leader either contributes to burnout or works against it. Every culture either creates clarity or confusion. Every day, your actions are shaping whether people stay, leave, disengage, or speak up.

There is a direct connection between disengagement, apathy, poor communication, and your retention, rebooking, referrals, and revenue. When people feel overlooked or unimportant, it shows up in your numbers. It shows up in your reputation. It shows up in who comes back and who quietly disappears.

Sometimes the fix is simple. Clear expectations. Better training. A stronger feedback loop. But if your team is already checked out, none of that will stick.

That has to be addressed first. If you ignore it, it will cost you more than talent. It will cost you trust.

Ask yourself:

- Do people feel safe giving honest feedback, or just saying what they think I want to hear?
- Are we rewarding loyalty, or just expecting it?
- Are we pushing for output while ignoring the cost to the people producing it?
- Are we building an environment where both performance and well-being are non-negotiable?
- Do we make it easy for people to speak up early, or only when they are already done?

Culture is not what you say. It is what you tolerate. It is also what you ignore, excuse, or stay silent about. It is shaped by how you respond when someone is struggling, how you handle conflict, and how often you address the real issues instead of just the symptoms. Culture is what happens when no one is watching, and what people learn to expect from you over time.

You do not have to fix everything overnight. But it starts by having genuine conversations about more than just performance. Take time to understand the people behind the work. Ask about what motivates them, what challenges them, and what they care about. When you know more about who they are, not just what they do, you become a better leader. And when something shifts, when someone pulls back or their energy changes, you will notice it sooner.

Sometimes people are dealing with things in their personal life, and it shows up at work. Other times, they are carrying issues at work that go far beyond the everyday challenges we all learn to solve. It is your job as a leader to understand which one is happening, and to respond accordingly.

If someone on your team is showing signs of detachment, stop assuming they are the problem. Start listening. Ask better questions. Create space for the truth before the silence costs you everything.

This book is not a complaint. It is a mirror. What you do with it is up to you.

The moment is now. ◆

REFERENCES

American Institute of Stress. (n.d.). *50 common signs and symptoms of stress.* https://www.stress.org/stress-effects

American Psychological Association. (n.d.). *Work, stress and health & socioeconomic status.* https://www.apa.org

American Psychological Association. (2022). *Work and well-being survey results: Stress and identity in the workplace.* https://www.apa.org/news/press/releases/stress/2022/identity-workplace

American Psychological Association. (2023). *Workplace mental health.* https://www.apa.org/topics/mental-health/workplace

Angelou, M. (1986). *All God's children need traveling shoes.* Random House.

Bandura, A. (1977). Self-efficacy: *Toward a unifying theory of behavioral change. Psychological Review,* 84(2), 191–215.

Brach, T. (2003). *Radical acceptance: Embracing your life with the heart of a Buddha.* Bantam.

Bridges, W. (2004). *Transitions: Making sense of life's changes* (2nd ed.). Da Capo Press.

Brown, B. (2010). *The gifts of imperfection: Let go of who you think you're supposed to be and embrace who you are.* Hazelden Publishing.

Brown, B. (2012). *Daring greatly: How the courage to be vulnerable transforms the way we live, love, parent, and lead.* Gotham Books.

Brown, B. (2015). *Rising strong: How the ability to reset transforms the way we live, love, parent, and lead.* Spiegel & Grau.

Bryant, T. (2022). *Homecoming: Overcome fear and trauma to reclaim your whole, authentic self.* TarcherPerigee.

Burnett, B., & Evans, D. (2016). *Designing your life: How to build a well-lived, joyful life*. Knopf.

Chow, J., Heller, A., & Stewart, S. (2022, April 5). *Help your employees find purpose—or watch them leave*. McKinsey & Company. https://www.mckinsey.com/featured-insights

Coutu, D. L. (2002, May). *How resilience works*. Harvard Business Review, 80(5), 46– 55. https://hbr.org/2002/05/how-resilience-works

Coyle, D. (2018). *The culture code: The secrets of highly successful groups*. Bantam Books.

Csikszentmihalyi, M. (1990). *Flow: The psychology of optimal experience*. Harper & Row.

David, S. (2016). *Emotional agility: Get unstuck, embrace change, and thrive in work and life*. Avery.

Deci, E. L., & Ryan, R. M. (2000). *The "what" and "why" of goal pursuits: Human needs and the self-determination of behavior*. Psychological Inquiry, 11(4), 227–268. https://doi.org/10.1207/S15327965PLI1104_01

Duffy, M. K., Ganster, D. C., & Pagon, M. (2002). *Social undermining in the workplace*. Academy of Management Journal, 45(2), 331–351. https://doi.org/10.5465/3069350

Dweck, C. S. (2006). *Mindset: The new psychology of success*. Random House.

Edmondson, A. C. (1999). *Psychological safety and learning behavior in work teams*. Administrative Science Quarterly, 44(2), 350–383. https://doi.org/10.2307/2666999

Edmondson, A. C. (2019). *The fearless organization: Creating psychological safety in the workplace for learning, innovation, and growth.* Wiley.

Eger, E. (2020). *The gift: 12 lessons to save your life.* Scribner.

Eisenberger, R., Huntington, R., Hutchison, S., & Sowa, D. (2002). *Perceived organizational support. Journal of Organizational Behavior,* 13(1), 1–12. https://doi.org/10.1002/job.145

Emerson, R. W. (1841). *Self-reliance.* James Munroe and Company.

Eurich, T. (2018). *Insight: The surprising truth about how others see us, how we see ourselves, and why the answers matter more than we think.* Currency.

Frankl, V. E. (1959). *Man's search for meaning.* Beacon Press.

Gabriel, A. S., Koopman, J., Rosen, C. C., & Johnson, R. E. (2021). *Helping others at work: A daily diary study of the consequences of helping behavior. Journal of Applied Psychology,* 106(5), 679–698. https://doi.org/10.1037/apl0000814

Gallup. (2023). *State of the Global Workplace: 2023 Report.* Gallup, Inc.

Gorbatov, S., & Lane, A. (2020). *The organizational culture lie. Harvard Business Review.* https://hbr.org

Hülsheger, U. R., & Schewe, A. F. (2011). *On the costs and benefits of emotional labor: A meta-analysis of surface acting and deep acting outcomes. Journal of Applied Psychology,* 96(2), 377–392. https://doi.org/10.1037/a0023047

Lorde, A. (1988). *A burst of light: Essays.* Firebrand Books.

Maslow, A. H. (1943). *A theory of human motivation. Psychological Review,* 50(4), 370–396.

Maté, G., & Maté, D. (2022). *The myth of normal: Trauma, illness, and healing in a toxic culture.* Avery.

Pink, D. H. (2009). *Drive: The surprising truth about what motivates us.* Riverhead Books.

Pressfield, S. (2002). *The war of art: Break through the blocks and win your inner creative battles.* Black Irish Entertainment LLC.

Tawwab, N. G. (2021). *Set boundaries, find peace: A guide to reclaiming yourself.* TarcherPerigee.

Tedeschi, R. G., & Calhoun, L. G. (2004). *Posttraumatic growth: Conceptual foundations and empirical evidence. Psychological Inquiry,* 15(1), 1–18. https://doi.org/10.1207/s15327965pli1501_01

Tolle, E. (1997). *The power of now: A guide to spiritual enlightenment.* New World Library.

van der Kolk, B. (2014). *The body keeps the score: Brain, mind, and body in the healing of trauma.* Viking.

World Health Organization. (2019, May 28). *Burn-out an "occupational phenomenon":* International Classification of Diseases. https://www.who.int/mental_health/evidence/burn-out/en/

ABOUT THE AUTHOR

TJ Minson, M.A., is a global leadership strategist, author, and founder of Callidora Global Media, a consulting firm dedicated to enhancing employee and client experiences through strategy, storytelling, and emotional intelligence.

With a Bachelor's in Business Administration and a Master's in Organizational Leadership specializing in Training and Development, TJ has always been driven by a fascination with psychology and a commitment to understanding what truly motivates individuals and teams. He chose Organizational Leadership instead of a psychology degree because he wanted something more applied, more human, and more aligned with the way people actually work inside organizations. His Master's capstone project in 2011 laid the foundation for this deep exploration into workplace engagement, identity, and organizational dynamics, receiving encouragement for publication early on. Over the years, extensive international travel and experience leading cross-functional teams further enriched TJ's global perspective, equipping him to understand the profound impact leadership decisions have on organizational culture and performance.

Today, TJ partners with a wide range of organizations, applying rigorous data analysis to uncover patterns in customer journeys, client success, and retention performance. His work highlights the critical connection between employee engagement and business outcomes. With an approach that is both research-informed and results-driven, TJ consistently helps organizations improve retention, engagement, and operational effectiveness.

In addition to his consulting expertise, TJ is an accomplished author of ten children's books, skillfully merging STEM and social-emotional learning (SEL) to empower young readers to understand the world around them and navigate their emotional lives.

Notable titles include:

- *What's That Cloud? A Kid's Guide to Real Cloud Types and the Feelings They Can Reflect*
- *Why Does the Moon Look Like That? A Kid's Guide to Real Moon Phases and the Feelings They Can Reflect*
- *Where Did the Star Go?*, a compassionate guide to grief for children
- *The Adventures of Mae the Elephant*, a beloved fiction series translated into six languages and enjoyed by readers in over 30 countries.

TJ's latest book, *How to Enjoy Work When You Hate Your Job*, is a culmination of years of academic research, personal observation, and professional insights into workplace dynamics. It provides practical strategies for professionals navigating burnout, disengagement, and workplace frustration, with the aim of restoring energy, clarity, and control.

Still feeling stuck or ready to lead differently?

Visit callidoraglobalmedia.com to connect with TJ, explore his books, and learn how his consulting work helps individuals and organizations rebuild trust, retention, and clarity at work.

If you lead a team and want to explore tools and insights designed to strengthen engagement and performance, visit callidoraglobalmedia.com/insights